THE BEST OF
ONE DIRECTION

WISE PUBLICATIONS
PART OF THE MUSIC SALES GROUP
LONDON / NEW YORK / PARIS / SYDNEY / COPENHAGEN / BERLIN / MADRID / HONG KONG / TOKYO

Published by
Wise Publications
14-15 Berners Street, London W1T 3LJ, UK.

Exclusive Distributors
Music Sales Limited
Distribution Centre, Newmarket Road,
Bury St Edmunds, Suffolk IP33 3YB, UK.
Music Sales Pty Limited
Units 3-4, 17 Willfox Street, Condell Park,
NSW 2200, Australia.

Order No. AM1007787
ISBN: 978-1-78305-351-3
This book © Copyright 2013 Wise Publications,
a division of Music Sales Limited.

Compiled and edited by Jenni Norey.
Music arranged by Vasco Hexel.
Music processed by Paul Ewers Music Design.
Cover design by Tim Field.
Cover photograph - Dave Hogan/Getty Images.
Inside Photographs - Mike Marsland/WireImage,
Samir Hussein/Redferns via Getty Images, Dave Hogan/Getty Images.

Printed in the EU.

THE BEST OF
ONE DIRECTION

Within a space of just three years, One Direction have made history with their chart-topping success around the world.

They have barely paused for breath since being formed on the TV talent show *The X Factor* in 2010 and there's still no respite with a world stadium tour booked for 2014 that will seal their world domination.

When their debut album *Up All Night* topped the charts in both the UK and the USA, even jaded music journalists took notice. Not even The Beatles had managed to achieve that.

The five band members – Harry, Liam, Niall, Louis and Zayn – were startled by the hysteria they caused amongst female fans in each country they visited. It seemed like only yesterday they were just normal teenage 'wannabes'. Now they had become the biggest band in the world.

LOUIS spent his first paycheck on adopting a chimpanzee called Larry, and admits he's a bit of monkey himself being the messiest member of the band! He's also a keen footballer, joining Doncaster Rovers as a non-contract player in 2013.

HARRY counts his most recognisable features and habits as his curly hair, dimples, trademark blazer and being flirtatious and cheeky. Don't approach Harry with any goats or snakes however, he's terrified of them! As well as being a member of One Direction and a modern-day pop icon, Harry is also a fan of knitting and a skilled kazoo player.

ZAYN was born Zain, but he decided to change the spelling due to liking how it looked written down. Like Liam, Harry and Louis, he has a number of tattoos including one in tribute to his Arabic grandfather, Walter, who passed away while he was on *The X Factor.* When translated from Arabic, Zayn means beautiful.

NIALL is One Direction's Irish connection, born in Mullingar, Ireland. His signature blonde hair is in fact dyed, as Niall's natural hair colour is brown. He is a keen guitarist, citing his guitar as the best Christmas present he has ever received.

LIAM is said to be the most competitive member of the band. He studied Music Technology at college and first entered *The X Factor* in 2008 aged just 14. After the age limit for entry was raised to 16, he was made to wait before he had the chance to try again, when he signed up for the 2010 series, eventually becoming a member of One Direction.

Best Song Ever

Words & Music by Wayne Hector, John Ryan,
Julian Bunetta & Edward Drewett

1. May - be it's the way she walked _____ straight in - to my heart and stole
2. Said her name was Geor - gia Rose _____ and her dad - dy was a den -

12

Change My Mind

Words & Music by Savan Kotecha, Carl Falk
& Rami Yacoub

Gotta Be You

Words & Music by Steve Mac & August Rigo

And no wom-an in the world de-serves_ this; but here I am, ask-ing you for

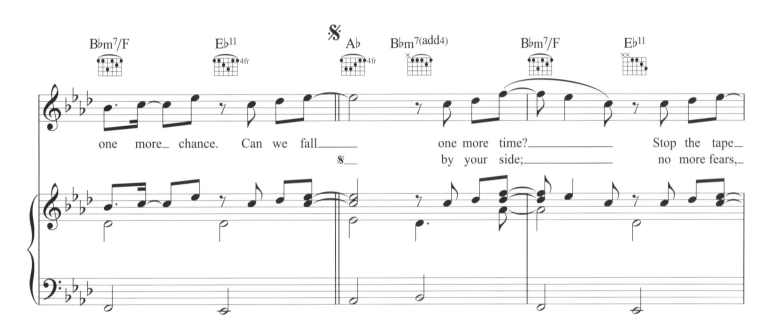

one more_ chance. Can we fall_____ one more time?_____ Stop the tape_
&_ by your side;_____ no more fears,_

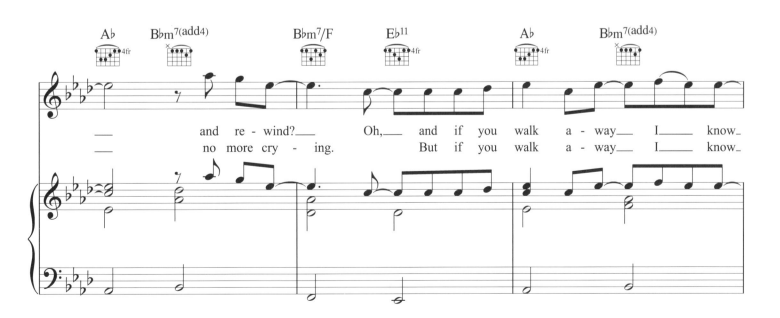

____ and re-wind?____ Oh,____ and if you walk a-way____ I____ know_
____ no more cry-ing. But if you walk a-way____ I____ know_

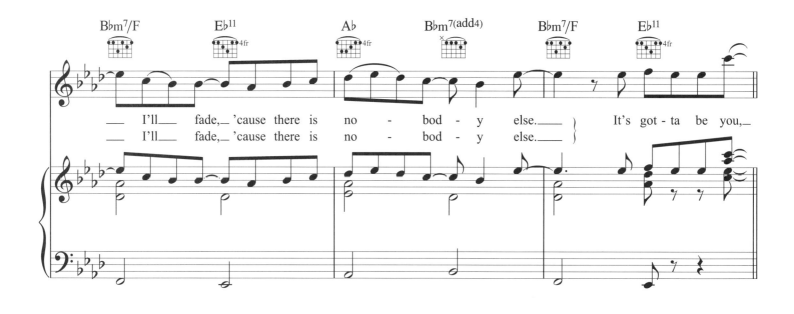

I'll__ fade,__ 'cause there is no - bod - y else.__ It's got-ta be you,__

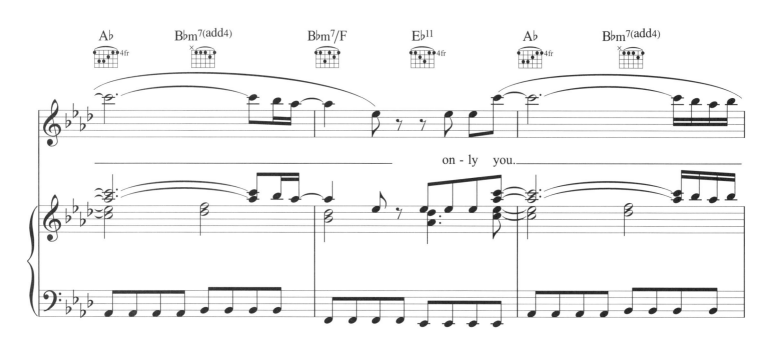

on - ly you.__

It's got to be you,_____ on - ly you.__

D.S. al Coda   ⊕ **Coda**

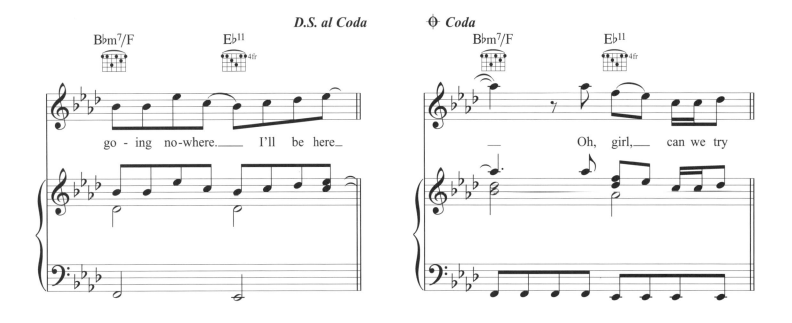

go- ing no-where.___ I'll be here___   Oh, girl,___ can we try

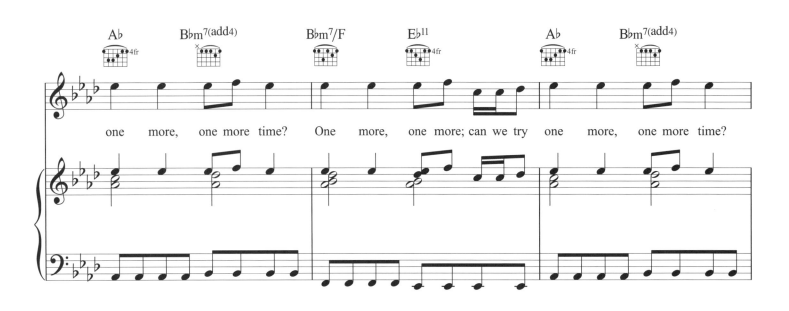

one more, one more time? One more, one more; can we try one more, one more time?

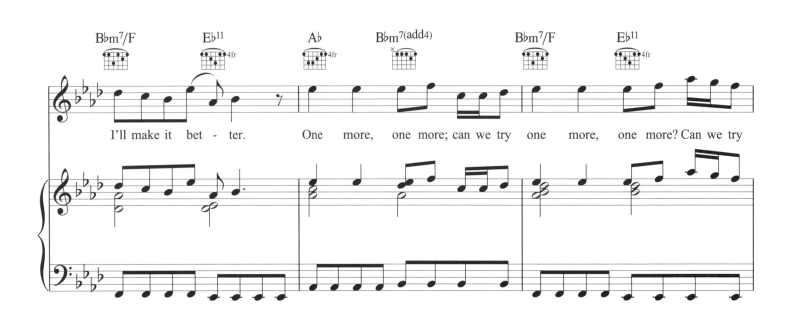

I'll make it bet - ter. One more, one more; can we try one more, one more? Can we try

22

only you.

It's got-ta be you, on - ly you.

Repeat to fade

Kiss You

*Words & Music by Savan Kotecha, Kristian Lundin, Carl Falk, Rami Yacoub,
Shellback, Kristoffer Fogelmark & Albin Nedler*

(Let me kiss___ you.) (Let me kiss___ you.)

(Let me kiss___ you.) (Let me kiss___ you.)
Come on!

Na, na, na, na, na, na, na, na.___ Na, na, na, na, na, na, na, na.___

Na, na, na, na, na, na, na, na.___ So tell me, girl, if ev-'ry time___ we___
Yeah!

Last First Kiss

Words & Music by Savan Kotecha, Carl Falk, Rami Yacoub, Kristoffer Fogelmark,
Albin Nedler, Liam Payne, Zain Malik & Louis Tomlinson

1. Ba-by, I, I wan-na know what you think when you're a-lone. Is it me?
2. Ba-by, tell me would it change? I'm a-fraid you'll run a-way. If I tell

— Yeah. Are you think-ing of me? — Yeah, oh.
— you what I've want-ed to tell — you. Yeah.

Little Things

Words & Music by Ed Sheeran & Fiona Bevan

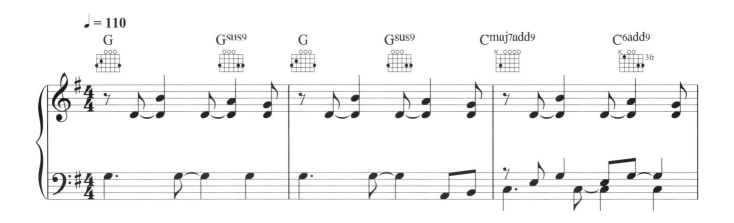

1. Your hand fits in mine like it's made___ just for me. But

2. I know you've nev-er___ loved the crin-kles by your eyes when you smile.___

Live While We're Young

Words & Music by Savan Kotecha, Carl Falk
& Rami Yacoub

43

Moments

Words & Music by Ed Sheeran & Simon Hulbert

50

your life,   your   voice,   your rea - son to be.

My love,   my   heart,   is breath - ing for this

mo - ment in   time.   I'll find the words to say

be - fore you leave me to - day.
(You know I'll be...)

More Than This

Words & Music by Jamie Scott

56

I've nev-er had___ the words___ to say,___ but now I'm ask - ing you___ to stay___
And as you close___ your eyes___ to - night,___ I pray that you___ will see___ the light___

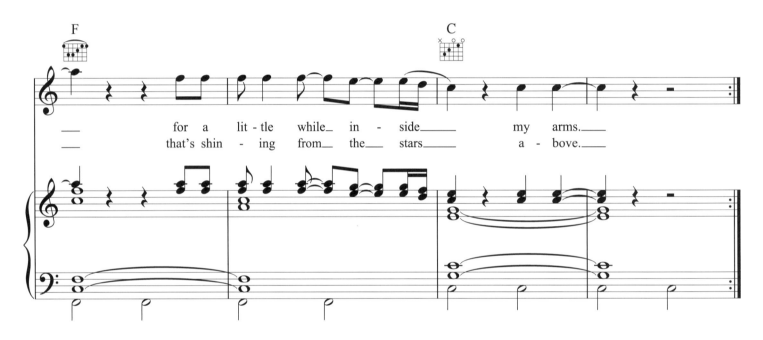

___ for a lit - tle while___ in - side___ my arms.___
___ that's shin - ing from___ the___ stars___ a - bove.___

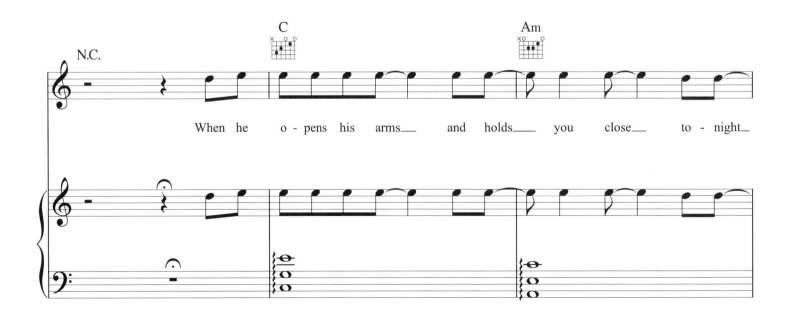

When he o - pens his arms___ and holds___ you close___ to - night___

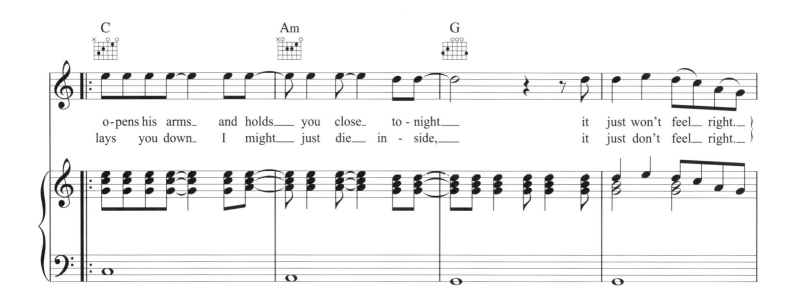

o-pens his arms___ and holds___ you close___ to - night___ it just won't feel___ right.___
lays you down___ I might___ just die___ in - side,___ it just don't feel___ right.___

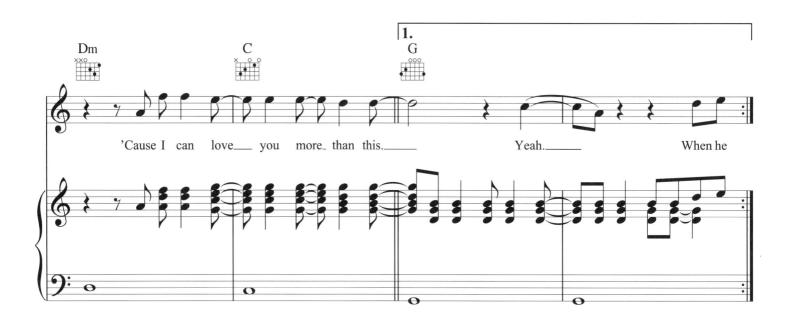

'Cause I can love___ you more_ than this.___ Yeah.___ When he

___ Can love___ you more_ than___ this.

One Thing

Words & Music by Savan Kotecha, Carl Falk
& Rami Yacoub

2. Shot me out of the sky. You're my kryp-to-nite._____
3. Now I'm climb-ing the walls, but you don't no-tice at___ all,_____ that

You keep mak-ing me___ weak._____ Yeah, fro-zen___ and can't breathe.__ Some -
I'm go-ing out of my___ mind_____ all day___ and all night.__ Some -

- thing's got-ta give now,_____ 'cause I'm dy - ing just to make you see. That I need_
- thing's got-ta give now._____ 'cause I'm dy - ing just to know your name. And I need_

___ you here with me now._____ 'Cause you've got___ that one___ thing.}
___ you here with me now._____ 'Cause you've got___ that one___ thing.} So

62

One Way Or Another (Teenage Kicks)

Words & Music by John O'Neill, Deborah Harry
& Nigel Harrison

72

Rock Me

Words & Music by Peter Svensson, Lukasz Gottwald,
Henry Russell Walter, Sam Hollander & Allan Grigg

Fm E♭ D♭maj9 A♭ Fm E♭
6fr 4fr 6fr
rock me, rock me, rock me, yeah. I want you to rock me, rock me,
D♭maj9 A♭ Fm E♭ D♭maj9 A♭
4fr 6fr 4fr
rock me, yeah. I want you to hit the pe-dal, heav-y me-tal, show me you care. I want you to
1. 2.
Fm E♭ D♭maj9 A♭ D♭maj9 A♭
6fr 4fr 4fr
rock me, rock me, rock me, yeah. 3. Yeah, rock me, yeah.
Fm E♭ D♭maj9 A♭ Fm E♭
6fr 4fr 6fr
R-O-C-K me a-gain. R-O-C-K me a-gain. R-O-C-K me a-

Summer Love

Words & Music by Wayne Hector, Guy Chambers, Stephen Robson, Lindy Robbins,
Niall Horan, Liam Payne, Zain Malik & Louis Tomlinson

Yeah.

Oh.   Oh,   oh.

1. Can't be - lieve____ you're____ pack-ing your____ bags____ try-ing so____ hard not____
2. Wish that we____ could____ be a - lone____ now____ if we could find some place____

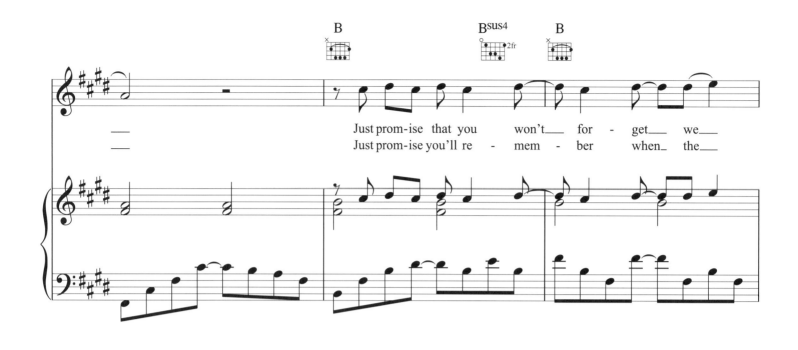

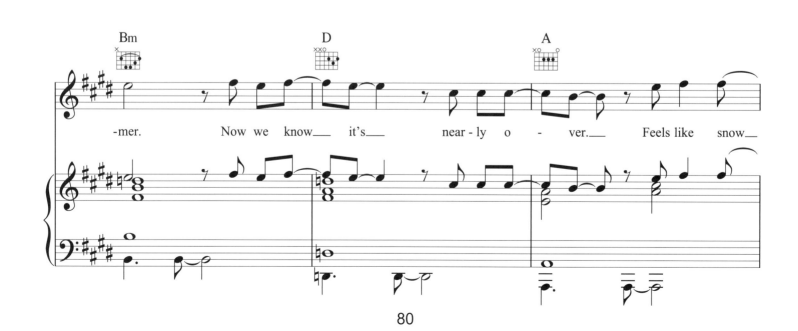

in Sep-tem - ber___ but I al - ways___ will re-mem - ber___ you were my___

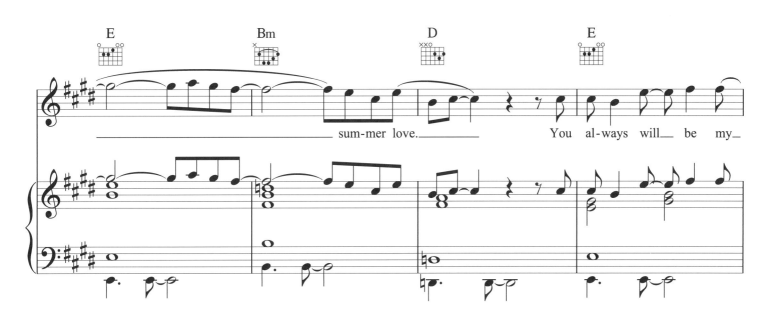

_____ sum-mer love._____ You al-ways will___ be my___

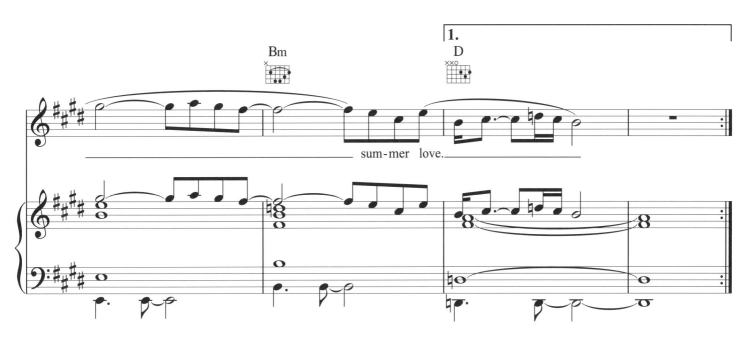

_____ sum-mer love.___

So please don't__ make__ this an-y hard-er. We can't__ take__ this an-y far-ther. And I__ know__ there's noth-ing that I__ wan-na change,__ change.__ 'Cause you were mine__ for the sum-mer. Now we know__

What Makes You Beautiful

Words & Music by Savan Kotecha, Carl Falk
& Rami Yacoub

They Don't Know About Us

Words & Music by Tommy James, Peter Wallevik,
Tebey Ottoh & Tommy Gregersen

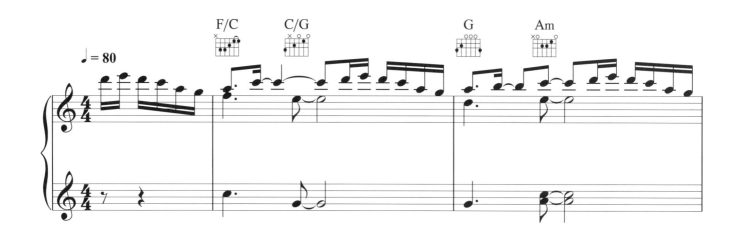

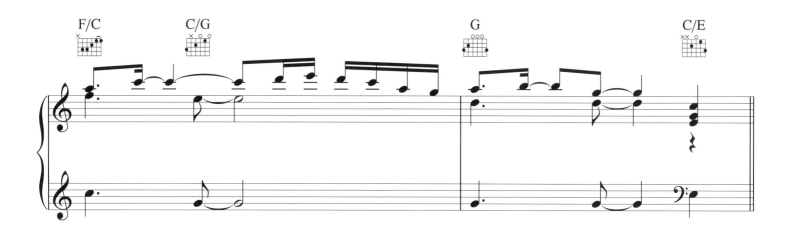

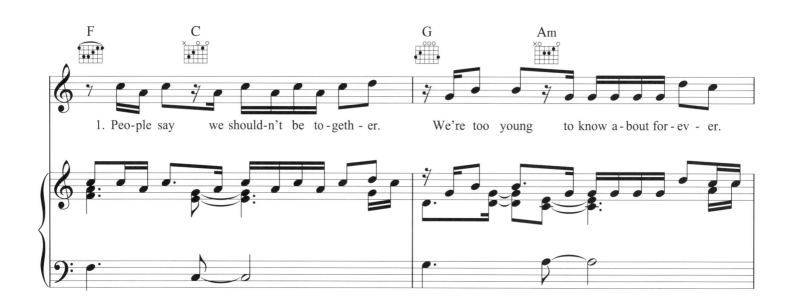

1. Peo-ple say we should-n't be to-geth-er. We're too young to know a-bout for-ev-er.

But I wan-na tell 'em, I wan-na tell the world that you're mine, girl. They don't know a-bout the

things we__ do. They don't know a-bout the I love__ yous. But I bet you if they

on - ly__ knew they would just be jea-lous of us. They don't know a-bout the